Notes on Grief

Notes on Grief

Chimamanda Ngozi Adichie

ALFRED A. KNOPF

NEW YORK TORONTO 2021

THIS IS A BORZOI BOOK
PUBLISHED BY ALFRED A. KNOPF
AND ALFRED A. KNOPF CANADA

All rights reserved. Published in the United States by
Alfred A. Knopf, a division of Penguin Random House LLC,
New York, and in Canada by Alfred A. Knopf Canada, a division
of Penguin Random House Canada Limited, Toronto.

www.aaknopf.com
www.penguinrandomhouse.ca

Knopf, Borzoi Books, and the colophon are registered trademarks
of Penguin Random House LLC. Knopf Canada and colophon are
trademarks of Penguin Random House Canada Limited.

This is a slightly expanded version of a piece written by the author that
originally appeared in *The New Yorker* on September 10, 2020.

Library of Congress Control Number: 2021931412
ISBN 978-0-593-32080-8 (hardcover)
ISBN 978-0-593-32081-5 (ebook)

Library and Archives Canada data is available upon request
Hardcover 9781039001558
EL 9781039001565

Jacket painting © Lossapardo
Jacket design by Joan Wong

Manufactured in the United States of America

First Edition

IN MEMORIAM

James Nwoye Adichie

1932–2020

Notes on Grief

I

From England, my brother set up the Zoom calls every Sunday, our boisterous lockdown ritual: two siblings joining from Lagos, three of us from the United States, and my parents, sometimes echoing and crackly, from Abba, our ancestral hometown in southeastern Nigeria. On 7 June, there was my father, only his forehead on the screen, as usual, because he never quite knew how to hold his phone during video calls. "Move your phone a bit, Daddy," one of us would say. My father was teasing my brother Okey about a new nickname, then he was saying he hadn't had dinner because they'd had a late lunch, then he was talking about the billionaire from the next town who wanted to claim our village's ancestral land. He felt a bit unwell, had been sleeping poorly, but we were not to worry. On 8 June, Okey went to Abba to see him and said he looked tired. On 9 June, I kept our chat brief, so that he could rest. He laughed quietly when I did my playful imitation of a relative. "*Ka chi fo*," he said. Good night. His last words to me. On 10 June, he was gone. My brother Chuks called to tell me, and I came undone.

2

My four-year-old daughter says I scared her. She gets down on her knees to demonstrate, her small clenched fist rising and falling, and her mimicry makes me see myself as I was: utterly unraveling, screaming and pounding the floor. The news is like a vicious uprooting. I am yanked away from the world I have known since childhood. And I am resistant: my father read the newspaper that afternoon, he joked with Okey about shaving before his appointment with the kidney specialist in Onitsha the next day, he discussed his hospital test results on the phone with my sister Ijeoma, who is a doctor—and so how can this be? But there he is. Okey is holding a phone over my father's face, and my father looks asleep, his face relaxed, beautiful in repose. Our Zoom call is beyond surreal, all of us weeping and weeping and weeping, in different parts of the world, looking in disbelief at the father we adore now lying still on a hospital bed. It happened a few minutes before midnight, Nigerian time, with Okey by his side and Chuks on speakerphone. I stare and stare at my father. My breathing is difficult. Is this what shock means, that the air turns to glue? My sister Uche says she has just told a family friend by text, and I almost scream, "No!

Don't tell anyone, because if we tell people, then it becomes true." My husband is saying, "Breathe slowly, drink some of this water." My housecoat, my lockdown staple, is lying crumpled on the floor. Later my brother Kene will jokingly say, "You better not get any shocking news in public, since you react to shock by tearing off your clothes."

3

~

Grief is a cruel kind of education. You learn how ungentle mourning can be, how full of anger. You learn how glib condolences can feel. You learn how much grief is about language, the failure of language and the grasping for language. Why are my sides so sore and achy? It's from crying, I'm told. I did not know that we cry with our muscles. The pain is not surprising, but its physicality is: my tongue unbearably bitter, as though I ate a loathed meal and forgot to clean my teeth; on my chest, a heavy, awful weight; and inside my body, a sensation of eternal dissolving. My heart—my actual physical heart, nothing figurative here—is running away from me, has become its own separate thing, beating too fast, its rhythms at odds with mine. This is an affliction not merely of the spirit but of the body, of aches and lagging strength. Flesh, muscles, organs are all compromised. No physical position is comfortable. For weeks, my stomach is in turmoil, tense and tight with foreboding, the ever-present certainty that somebody else will die, that more will be lost. One morning, Okey calls me a little earlier than usual and I think, *Just tell me, tell me immediately, who has died now. Is it Mummy?*

In my American home, I like to have National Public Radio on as background noise, and whenever my father was staying he would turn it off if nobody was there listening to it.

"I just thought about how Daddy was always turning off the radio and I was always turning it back on. He probably thought it was wasteful in some way," I tell Okey.

"Like he always wanted to turn off the generator too early in Abba. I'd so happily let him now if he'll just come back," Okey says, and we laugh.

"And I will start to wake up early and I'll start to eat *garri* and I'll go to Mass every Sunday," I say, and we laugh.

I retell the story of my parents visiting me in my graduate-student apartment at Yale, when I say, "Daddy, will you have some pomegranate juice?" and he says, "No, thank you, whatever that is."

Pomegranate juice became a standing joke. All those standing jokes we had, frequently told and retold, my father's expression one minute utterly deadpan and, the next, wide open with delighted laughter. Another revelation: how much laughter is a part of grief. Laughter is tightly braided into our family argot, and now we laugh remembering my father, but somewhere in the background there is a haze of disbelief. The laughter trails off. The laughter becomes tears and becomes sadness and becomes rage. I am unprepared for my wretched, roaring rage. In the face of this inferno that is sorrow, I am callow and unformed. But how can it be that in the morning he is joking and talking, and at night he is gone forever? It was so fast, too fast. It was not supposed to happen like this, not like a malicious surprise, not during a pandemic that has shut down the world. Throughout the lockdown, my father and I talked about how strange it all was, how scary, and he told me often not to worry about my doctor husband. "You actually drink warm water, Daddy?" I asked one day, surprised, laughing at him, after he said, with sheepish humor, that he'd read somewhere that drinking warm water might prevent coronavirus. He laughed at himself and told me warm water was harmless, after all. It was not like the nonsense that went around during the Ebola scare, when people were bathing in saline before dawn. To my "How are you, Daddy?" he would always respond, "*Enwerom nsogbu chacha*." I have no problems at all. I'm perfectly fine. And he really was. Until he wasn't.

5

Messages pour in and I look at them as through a mist. Who is this message for? "On the loss of your father," one says. Whose father? My sister forwards a message from her friend that says my father was humble despite his accomplishments. My fingers start to tremble and I push my phone away. He *was* not; he *is*. There is a video of people trooping into our house for *mgbalu*, to give condolences, and I want to reach in and wrench them away from our living room, where already my mother is settled on the sofa in placid widow pose. A table is in front of her like a barrier, to maintain social distance. Already friends and relatives are saying this must be done and that must be done. A condolence register must be placed by the front door, so my sister goes off to buy a bolt of white lace to cover the table and my brother buys a hardcover notebook and soon people are bending to write in the book. I think, *Go home! Why are you coming to our house to write in that alien notebook? How dare you make this thing true?* Somehow, these well-wishers have become complicit. I feel myself breathing air that is bittersweet with my own conspiracies. Needle-pricks of resentment flood through me at the thought of people who are more than eighty-eight years old, older than my father and alive and well. My anger scares me, my fear scares me, and somewhere in there is shame, too—why am I so enraged and so scared? I am afraid of going to bed and of waking up; afraid of tomorrow and of all the tomorrows after. I am filled with disbelieving astonishment that the mailman comes as usual and that people are inviting me to speak somewhere and that regular news alerts appear on my phone screen. How is it that the world keeps going, breathing in and out unchanged, while in my soul there is a permanent scattering?

6

Grief is forcing new skins on me, scraping scales from my eyes. I regret my past certainties: *Surely you should mourn, talk through it, face it, go through it.* The smug certainties of a person yet unacquainted with grief. I have mourned in the past, but only now have I touched grief's core. Only now do I learn, while feeling for its porous edges, that there is no way through. I am in the center of this churning, and I have become a maker of boxes, and inside their unbending walls I cage my thoughts. I torque my mind firmly to its shallow surface alone. I cannot think too much, I dare not think too deeply, or else I will be defeated, not merely by pain but by a drowning nihilism, a cycle of thinking there's no point, what's the point, there's no point to anything. I want there to be a point, even if I do not know, for now, what that point is. There is a grace in denial, Chuks says, words that I repeat to myself. A refuge, this denial, this refusal to look. Of course, the effort is its own grieving, and so I am unlooking in the oblique shadow of looking, but imagine the catastrophe of a direct, unswerving stare. Often, too, there is the urge to run and run, to hide. But I cannot always run, and each time I am forced to squarely confront my grief—when I read the death certificate, when I draft a death announcement—I feel a shimmering panic. In such moments, I notice a curious physical reaction: my body begins to shake, fingers tap uncontrollably, one leg bobbing. I am unable to quiet myself until I look away. How do people walk around functioning in the world after losing a beloved father? For the first time in my life, I am enamored of sleeping pills, and, in the middle of a shower or a meal, I burst into tears.

7

My wariness of superlatives is forever stripped away: 10 June 2020 was the worst day of my life. There is such a thing as the worst day of a life, and please, dear universe, I do not want anything ever to top it. In the week before 10 June, while running around playing with my daughter, I fell and hit my head and suffered a concussion. For days, I felt unmoored, sensitive to sound and light. I did not call my parents daily as usual. When I finally called, my father wanted to talk, not about his feeling unwell but about my head. Concussions can be slow to heal, he told me. "You just said 'concoction.' The word is 'concussion,'" my mother said from the background. I wish I had not missed those few days of calling them, because I would have seen that he wasn't just mildly unwell—or I would have sensed it if it wasn't obvious—and I would have insisted on hospital much sooner. I wish, I wish. The guilt gnaws at my soul. I think of all the things that could have happened and all the ways the world could be reshaped, to prevent what happened on 10 June, to make it un-happen. I worry about Okey, a stalwart, sensitive soul, whose burden weighs differently from ours because he is the one who was there. He agonizes about what else he could have done that night when my father started to show discomfort, telling him, "Help me sit up," and then saying, no, he would rather lie back down. He says my father prayed, calmly, quietly—what sounded like bits of the rosary in Igbo. Does it comfort me to hear this? Only to the extent that it must have comforted my father.

The cause was complications from kidney failure. An infection, the doctor said, had exacerbated his long-term kidney disease. But what infection? I wonder about the coronavirus, of course. Some journalists had come to our house to interview him a few weeks before, about the case of the billionaire who wanted to take our hometown's land—a dispute that consumed my father these past two years. Might he have been exposed then? The doctor doesn't think so, even though he was not tested, because he would have had symptoms, and nobody else around him had symptoms. He needed hydration, and so he was admitted to the hospital and put on IV fluids. Okey stripped the tatty hospital bedsheets and replaced them with sheets he'd brought from home. The next day, 11 June, was my father's appointment with the kidney specialist.

8

Because I loved my father so much, so fiercely, so tenderly, I always, at the back of my mind, feared this day. But, lulled by his relative good health, I thought we had time. I thought it was not yet time. "I was so sure Daddy was nineties material," my brother Kene says. We all were. Perhaps we also unreasonably thought that his goodness, his being so decent, would keep him with us into his nineties. But did I sense a truth that I also fully denied? Did my spirit know— the way anxiety sat sharp like claws in my stomach once I heard he was unwell; my sleeplessness for two days; and the hovering darkening pall I could neither name nor shake off? I am the Family Worrier, but even for me it was extreme, how desperately I wished that Nigerian airports were open, so I could get a flight to Lagos and then to Asaba and drive the hour to my hometown to see my father for myself. So, I knew. I was so close to my father that I knew, without wanting to know, without fully knowing that I knew. A thing like this, dreaded for so long, finally arrives and among the avalanche of emotions there is a bitter and unbearable relief. It comes as a form of aggression, this relief, bringing with it strangely pugnacious thoughts. Enemies beware: the worst has happened. My father is gone. My madness will now bare itself.

9

How quickly my life has become another life, how pitiless this becoming is, and yet how slow I am to adapt. Okey sends me a video of an elderly woman who walks through our front door, crying, and I think, *I have to ask Daddy who she is.* In that small moment, what has been true for the forty-two years of my life is still true—that my father is tangible, inhaling, exhaling; reachable to talk to and to watch the twinkle of his eyes behind his glasses. Then, with a horrible lurch, I remember again. That brief forgetting feels like both a betrayal and a blessing. Do I forget because

I am not there? I think so. My brother and sister are there, face to face with the desolation of a house without my father. My sister kneeling by his bed, weeping. My brother wearing one of his newsboy hats, weeping. They can see that he is not at the dining table for breakfast, on his chair backing the window's light, and that after breakfast he is not settled on the sofa in his mid-morning ritual of napping, reading and napping again. If only I could be there too, but I am stuck in America, my frustration like a blister, scouring for news of when the Nigerian airports will open. Even the Nigerian authorities don't seem to know. A report says July, then August, then we hear it might be in October, but the aviation minister tweets to say "may be earlier than October." Maybe, maybe not, like playing yo-yo with a cat, only the stakes are people left in limbo because they cannot lay their beloved to rest.

I back away from condolences. People are kind, people mean well, but knowing this does not make their words rankle less. "Demise." A favorite of Nigerians, it conjures for me dark distortions. "On the demise of your father." I detest "demise." "He is resting" brings not comfort but a scoff that trails its way to pain. He could very well be resting in his room in our house in Abba, fan whirring warm air, his bed strewn with folded newspapers, a sudoku book, an old brochure from a funeral, a Knights of St. Mulumba calendar, a bag filled with his bottles of medicine, and his notebooks with the carefully lined pages on which he recorded every single thing he ate, a diabetic's account-taking. "He is in a better place" is startling in its presumptuousness, and has a taint of the inapt. How would you know—and shouldn't

I, the bereaved, be privy to this information first? Should I really be learning this from you? "He was eighty-eight" so deeply riles because age is irrelevant in grief; at issue is not how old he was but how loved. Yes, he was eighty-eight, but a cataclysmic hole now suddenly gapes open in your life, a part of you snatched away forever. "It has happened, so just celebrate his life," an old friend wrote, and it incensed me. How facile to preach about the permanence of death, when it is, in fact, the very permanence of death that is the source of anguish. I wince now at the words I said in the past to grieving friends. "Find peace in your memories," I used to say. To have love snatched from you, especially unexpectedly, and then to be told to turn to memories. Rather than succor, my memories bring eloquent stabs of pain that say, "This is what you will never again have." Sometimes they bring laughter, but laughter like glowing coals that soon burst aflame in pain. I hope that it is a question of time—that it is just too soon, too terribly soon, to expect memories to serve only as salve.

What does not feel like the deliberate prodding of wounds is a simple "I'm sorry," because in its banality it presumes nothing. *Ndo*, in Igbo, comforts more, a word that is "sorry" with a metaphysical heft, a word with borders wider than mere "sorry." Concrete and sincere memories from those who knew him comfort the most, and it warms me that the same words recur: "honest," "calm," "kind," "strong," "quiet," "simple," "peaceful," "integrity." My mother tells me that Ayogu called her to say that my father was the only boss who "never gave him any trouble." I remember Ayogu, tall with a genteel manner, my father's driver when he was deputy vice chancellor of the University of Nigeria, in the 1980s. Was it Ayogu or was it the other driver, Kevin, the charming firebrand, of whom my father once calmly said, when I had asserted, with the haughtiness of a seven-year-old, that I wanted my driver to take me to school, "He is *my* driver, not your driver."

II

❧

Grief is not gauzy; it is substantial, oppressive, a thing opaque. The weight is heaviest in the mornings, post-sleep: a leaden heart, a stubborn reality that refuses to budge. I will never see my father again. Never again. It feels as if I wake up only to sink and sink. In those moments, I am sure that I do not ever want to face the world again. Years ago, somebody died and a relative said with certainty, "The wife can't be alone," and I thought, *But what if she wants to be?* There is value in that Igbo way, that African way, of grappling with grief: the performative, expressive outward mourning, where you take every call and you tell and retell the story of what happened, where isolation is anathema and "stop crying" a refrain. But I am not ready. I talk only to my closest family. It is instinctive, my recoiling. I imagine the confusion of some relatives, their disapproval even, when faced with my withdrawal, the calls I leave unanswered, the messages unread. They might think it a mystifying self-indulgence or an affectation of fame, or both. In truth, at first it is a protective stance, a shrinking from further pain, because I am drained limp from crying, and to speak about it would be to cry again. But later it is because I want to sit alone with my grief. I want to protect—hide? hide from?—these foreign sensations, this bewildering series of hills and valleys. There is a desperation to shrug off this burden, and then a competing longing to cosset it, to hold it close. Is it possible to be possessive of one's pain? I want to become known to it, I want it known to me. So precious was my bond with my father that I cannot lay open my suffering until I have discerned its contours. One day I am in the bathroom, completely alone, and I call my father by my fond nickname for him—"the original dada"—and a brief blanket of peace enfolds me. Too brief. I am a person wary of the maudlin, but I am certain of this moment filled with my father. If it is a hallucination, then I want more of it, but it hasn't happened again.

12

My parents' cold-weather clothes hang in the closet of the guest room that my daughter calls "Grandpa and Grandma's room." I touch my father's puffy olive jacket. In the drawer are his maps of Maryland, just as he has maps of New England in a drawer in my sister's Connecticut home. During the months he and my mother spent every year in the U.S., he would study his beloved maps—the boundaries of counties, what was north and south of what—and trace every journey, even trips out to brunch. Scenes from my father's last visit: he is walking up and down the driveway, his daily morning exercise, no longer as briskly as before (his daily jog-walk slowed considerably at about the age of eighty-four), and he has decided to keep count with stones, and so we find a pile of stones near the front door. He is getting cookies in the pantry, blithely unaware of his trail of crumbs. He is standing right in front of the television, his code for "you all need to stop talking," watching Rachel Maddow, whom he calls "bright," while shaking his head at the imbroglio America has become.

13

I reread *Biography of Nigeria's Foremost Professor of Statistics, Prof. James Nwoye Adichie* by Emeritus

Professor Alex Animalu, Professor Peter I. Uche and Jeff Unaegbu, published in 2013, three years before my father was made professor emeritus of the University of Nigeria. The printing is uneven, the pages slightly askew, but I feel a euphoric rush of gratitude to the authors. Why does this line—"the children and I adore him"—from my mother's tribute in the book soothe me so? Why does it feel pacifying and prophetic? It pleases me that it exists, forever declared in print. I rummage in my study for the old letters he sent from Nigeria when I first came to the U.S. to attend college, and when I find them, there is an intense pathos to looking at his handwriting. It tells his story, that handwriting, the curvy script of a certain kind of colonial African education, prudent and proper, Latin-loving and rule-following. *Nnem ochie*, he called me. My grandmother. He always ended with "Your dad," and his signature. He wrote his signature even on our birthday cards, which made my siblings and me laugh. "Daddy, it's not a university memo," we'd say; "you don't have to write your signature." I look everywhere for the piece of paper on which he drew for me our family tree, going back four generations, but I cannot find it, and that I cannot find it causes me distress for days, boxes and files flung open, papers thrown aside.

I look at old photographs, and from time to time my whole body swells with a sob. My father often looked stiff in photos because he grew up knowing photography as a rare and formal event at which you dressed up and sat, uncomfortable, before a man with a tripod. "Daddy, relax. Daddy, smile." Sometimes I tried pinching his neck. There is a photo of him I remember taking. He is at our messy dining table in Nsukka, at the house on the campus of the University of Nigeria where I grew up, sitting on his chair, next to the chair that was my mother's chair. Our head-rubbing ritual began there. I was in secondary school when his bald patch first appeared, and I would come up behind him at the dining table and rub it, and he, without pausing in whatever he was saying, would gently slap my hand away.

I watch videos, saved on my computer, that feel like revelations because I do not remember them, even though I made some of them. We are having breakfast in my Lagos home and I am pretending to be a Nigerian journalist asking my father about his courtship with my mother, while he ignores me with a small smile on his face. We are in our house in Abba and my daughter, who is three years old, is crying because she wants to skip breakfast and play, and my father holds her and tells her nanny to take away the food and let her play.

~~~

In my study, I find his old sudoku books, the squares filled with his numbers, upright and confident, and I remember us driving to a bookshop in Maryland to buy them some years ago. He bought me one to try because "it's very good," but trying the first puzzle revived my hatred of mathematics. I remembered my father coaching me before I took my GCE exam and how he said, as I stalled in solving a long equation, "Yes, you're getting there. Don't doubt yourself. Don't stop." Is that why I believe now in always trying? It is, of course, too easy to draw simple causative lines. It was the wholeness of him that formed me, but it was also these incidents, slice by slice.

In secondary school, my friends and I once took a problem to the timid new mathematics teacher, Mr. O, and, glancing at the thorny problem, he hastily said he needed to go and get his four-figure table, even though the problem didn't require a four-figure table. We left his office roaring with the malicious mirth of teenagers. I told my father about this, expecting his laughter. But he didn't laugh. "The man is not a good teacher, not because he didn't know how to solve it, but because he didn't say he didn't know." Is that how I became a person confident enough to say I don't know when I don't know? My father taught me that learning is never-ending. He didn't have the entitlement that many Igbo parents of his generation have, that claim to their children's time and money and effort—which I suspect we would have forgiven anyway. But that he was so respectful of our boundaries, and so grateful for the smallest things, was like a priceless trimming.

Often I hailed him by his title "*Odelu-Ora Abba*," whose literal translation is "One Who Writes for Our Community." And he would hail me too, and his hailing me was a love-drenched litany of affirmation. "*Ome Ife Ukwu*" was the most common. "The One Who Does Great Things." I find the others difficult to translate: "*Nwoke Neli*" is roughly "The Equivalent of Many Men," and "*Ogbata Ogu Ebie*" is "The One Whose Arrival Ends the Battle." Is he the reason I have never been afraid of the disapproval of men? I think so.

15

No one was prepared for how deeply besotted with sudoku my father became after he retired, much to my mother's irritation.

"He won't eat," she would say, "because he's busy playing sudoku."

"You don't *play* sudoku," he would reply mildly. "It's not Ludo."

And I would quip, "James and Grace, bickering since 1963."

My mother's first words, when Okey walked into her room on the night of 10 June and turned on the light and told her, were "How can?"—Nigerian-speak for "It can't be, that's impossible, that can't be." And then she added the words that seared their way into our hearts on that Zoom call: "But he didn't tell me anything." Because he would have told her. They were like that. If he was going to leave us forever, he would have told her, and so his not having told her meant it could not be true. She had been in the hospital until a few hours before and had come home to get some sleep and then return for the trip to the kidney specialists in Onitsha. "I already brought out his sweater in case he gets cold," she said.

Their courting story charmed me. It began on a farm in 1960, with neither of them present. A relative of his was boasting about the bright young man who had just started teaching at a

34

university and was looking for an educated wife. A relative of hers said that she was educated and beautiful, fair as an egret. Fair as an egret! *O na-enwu ka ugbana!* Another standing family joke.

"Daddy, so you just get up and drive to a town you don't know to 'see' a girl you heard about?" I teased often. But that was how things were done. My mother liked his quietness. When her family at first resisted, because he wasn't as flashy or as wealthy as her other suitors, my mother said she would not marry anyone else. I called him DOS, Defender of Spouse, for how quick he always was to support my mother. One afternoon, when she was a deputy registrar—she later became the first woman to be the registrar at the University of Nigeria—he came home gleeful, chortling while loosening his tie, swollen with pride about her speech at the university senate meeting. "Mummy was fantastic," he told my brothers and me.

16

~

Okey tells me he slipped Daddy's watch into his pocket that night and he sends me a photo, the blue-faced silver watch that Kene bought him a few years ago. We were amused that my father started wearing it right away; we often bought him things that he never used because, he said, his shirt from 1970 or his shoes from 1985 were still perfectly fine. I keep looking at the photo of the watch, day after day, as if in pilgrimage. I remember it resting on my father's wrist, and my father often looking at it. This is an archetypal image of my father, his face bent to his watch, checking the time, a hyper-punctual man; for him, being on time was almost a moral imperative.

Childhood was my father downstairs on Sunday mornings, ready for Mass an hour before everyone else, walking up and down to hurry us up. In those years, he seemed remote. My mother was the warm, accessible parent, and he the man in the study writing statistics and talking to himself. I was vaguely proud of him. I might not have known that he was Nigeria's first professor of statistics, but I knew he had become a full professor long before the fathers of my friends, because there was a kid at school who called me "*Nwa Professor*," Professor's Child. In my later teenage years, I began to see him, to see how alike we were in our curiosity and our homebodyness, and to talk to him, and to adore him. How exquisitely he paid attention, how present he was, how well he listened. If you told him something, he remembered. His humor, already dry, crisped deliciously as he aged.

My best friend, Uju, tells me how my father turned to her at the end of my Harvard Class Day speech, in 2018, and, in a voice more powerful for being muted, said, "Look, they are all standing for her." I weep at this. Part of grief's tyranny is that it robs you of remembering the things that matter. His pride in me mattered, more than anyone else's. He read everything I wrote, and his comments ranged from "this isn't coherent at all" to "you have outdone yourself." Each time I traveled for speaking events, I would send him my itinerary and he would send texts to follow my progress. "You must be about to go onstage," he would write. "Go and shine. *Ome ife ukwu!*" Once, I was traveling to Denmark and, after wishing me a safe journey, he added, in his deadpan way, "And when you get to Denmark, look for Hamlet's house."

18

"You should just go and marry your father!" my cousin Oge said often, with mock exasperation, perhaps because one of my favorite things in the world was just to hang out with my father. To sit with him and talk about the past was like reclaiming gorgeous treasure that was always mine anyway. He gave me my ancestry in finely sketched stories. I not only adored him in that classic manner of a daddy's girl, but I also liked him so much. I *like* him. His grace and his wisdom and his simplicity, and how utterly unimpressionable he was. I liked his luminous, moderate faith, strong but worn lightly. If you expected my father to stay a weekend anywhere, you had to find the nearest Roman Catholic church. When I first moved to Maryland, I worried that St. John the Evangelist, in an inter-faith center in Columbia, with a guitar-playing choir, would be off-putting to him, nothing like his stained-glass Catholicism, but he pronounced the priest "very good" and happily went every Sunday. I liked that his response to power was a shrug. He worshipped integrity. He was indifferent to, if not distrustful of, grand flourishes.

"I have eight cars," my sister's wealthy suitor once boasted, and my father replied, "Why?"

He was not materialistic, and this would not be so remarkable if he were not a Nigerian living in Nigeria, with its hard-nosed grasping ethos, its untrammeled acquisitiveness from bottom to top. We are all blighted to different degrees, but he alone was wholly uninfected. I liked his sense of duty. There was something in his nature that was capacious, a spirit that could stretch; he absorbed bad news; he negotiated, compromised, made decisions, laid down rules, held relatives together. Much of it was the result of being born the first son in an Igbo family and having risen to its mesh of expectations and dispensations. He infused meaning into the simplest of descriptions: a good man, a good father. I liked to call him "a gentle man and a gentleman."

I liked, too, his appreciation for the properness of things. His meticulous record-keeping, the rows of files in his cabinet. Each child had files for primary, secondary and university records, and every domestic helper who ever lived with us had a file. Once, in the middle of watching an American newscast, he turned to me and asked, "What does this word 'nuke' mean?" And when I told him, he said, "Nuclear weapons are too serious to be given nicknames."

"You have a particular laugh when you're with Daddy," my husband tells me, "even when what he says isn't funny." I recognize the high-pitched cackle he mimics, and I know it is not so much about what my father says as it is about being with him. A laugh that I will never laugh again. "Never" has come to stay. "Never" feels so unfairly punitive. For the rest of my life, I will live with my hands outstretched for things that are no longer there.

19

Last Christmas, at a house-warming party in my sister Ijeoma's country home, my father was the patriarch and cynosure, seated in the middle of the living room, blessing the kola nut, sipping a little champagne, even though he hardly drank, and telling stories. Relatives arrived and went straight to pay him homage. He received a WhatsApp message sometime that afternoon but said nothing about it until we were back home, at night. He handed me his phone and said, "Read this. It appears this man has truly gone mad."

"This man" was the billionaire out to seize the vast expanse of ancestral land that belongs to my hometown, Abba. Land is the jewel of Igbo cosmology, and who owns land is often about stories: whose grandfather's grandfather farmed it, which clan migrated and which was indigenous. Land is also the thorn in so many disputes; I know of extended families torn apart fighting over a piece of land not big enough to park a car on. The land in question has been farmed by Abba people for decades, but, at the end of the Biafran war, with the whole of Igboland in disarray, an old order gone and a new one yet to be formed, the town next to ours suddenly claimed that it was theirs. Abba went to court, and the case has been tied up for years. Many people in Abba believed the billionaire was responsible for the arbitrary arrests and detention of villagers, to scare the town into giving up its claim to the land. A market was bulldozed. Compound walls were broken. (His brother disputed the claims in an interview with *The Guardian*.) Nobody in Abba was close to having the wealth and political connections of the billionaire, but there was a straight-talking businessman, Ikemba Njikoka, who was funding my hometown's legal expenses and speaking publicly about the billionaire's conduct. He himself had been threatened. The WhatsApp message on my father's phone had been forwarded by Ikemba Njikoka, saying that "you" would be arrested at a town hall meeting this weekend.

My father, not WhatsApp savvy, did not realize that it was a forwarded message and thought that *he* was about to be illegally arrested. He had spent the day silently burdened by this.

"Daddy, you should have said something earlier," I said.

"I didn't want to spoil Ijeoma's day," he said.

It angers me that my father's last months were blighted by the actions of a diminutive self-styled philanthropist drunk on oil wealth and bereft of scruples. It angers me, how worried I was for my parents' safety, especially in late 2019, when the billionaire began a brazen campaign against my hometown. "This is *wrong*," my father said often, with a moral shiver, as though it were unfathomable that a wealthy Nigerian man would act this way. Just as when it came to exam malpractice—a phenomenon so common in Nigeria as to be ordinary—each occurrence my father heard about left him newly appalled. His was a kind of naïveté, an innocence of the just. When my brothers and I surprised him on his eightieth birthday, arriving at our parents' flat in Nsukka from the U.S. and the UK, he kept looking at my mother in bafflement that she could have "lied" to him. "But you said some friends were coming. You didn't say the children were coming."

"No, Daddy: she wasn't allowed to say. That's what a surprise is."

20

"Mama is sad because Grandpa died," my four-year-old daughter says to her cousin. "Died." She knows the word "died." She pulls tissues out of a box and hands them to me. Her emotional alertness moves, surprises, impresses me. A few days later she asks, "When will Grandpa wake up again?"

I weep and weep, and wish that her understanding of the world were real. That grief was not about the utter impossibility of return.

One morning I am watching a video of my father on my phone, and my daughter glances at my screen and then swiftly places her hand over my eyes. "I don't want you to watch the video of Grandpa, because I don't want you to cry," she says. She is hawk-eyed in her vigilance of my tears.

"You'll always remember what Grandpa called you?" I ask her.

"Yes, Mama. *Ezigbo nwa*," she says. Good child, a translation made more inadequate for being literal.

I will tell her how much he delighted in her, his eighth grandchild; how pleased he was that she was being raised bilingual; how my husband and I joked that Grandpa would punish us if we upset her. A scene from my daughter's first months: my father is hurrying upstairs, my daughter is a howling baby downstairs in my mother's care. He has been sent up for the pacifier, whose name he does not remember, and so he urgently gestures to his mouth and tells me, "Mouth plug!" Months later, my daughter's potty training has passed the milestone of pee, and now she has been cajoled to sit on the potty and do more than pee, a rapt audience of family watching her, and my father wanders in and mildly asks, "Would any of *you* go if you had so many people watching you?"

21

The dictates of Igbo culture, this immediate pivot from pain to planning. Just the other day my father was on our Zoom call, and now, on this Zoom call, we are supposed to plan. To plan is to appease the egos of church and traditional groups and get a burial date approved, which cannot be during the New Yam Festival, or any other community ceremonial, and must be a Friday, because the parish priest buries the elderly only on Fridays. But the most important thing is "clearance"— it is a word thrown about in English, "clearance." Clearance attests to how deeply, how forcefully communitarian Igbo culture remains. Clearance means that any outstanding dues to the age grade, the town union, the village, the clan, the *umunna*, must be paid; otherwise, the funeral will be boycotted. A potent threat, the shunning of a funeral. To most Igbo people, at least those of my father's generation, to be deprived of a proper funeral is an almost existential fear. It is common to hear stories of grieving families outraged by the manipulation of village groups who ask for money, this their only chance to exercise a trifling power. My father was diligent with dues, so Okey runs around to get all the receipts. There are long lists of what each group expects from us: the age grades, the *umuada*, the traditional association of the town's women, the Catholic groups, the council of chiefs, the vigilante members who guard our town. How many coolers of rice, whether a gift of a chicken or a goat will be presented, how many cartons of beer. I look at the lists askance. It's not a bloody party. I don't care what we wear or what the caterer cooks or what groups come or don't come, because I am still sinking. But I have to care; these things mattered to my father. "Think of what Daddy would want," my brother Chuks says, comforting me.

My grandfather died in the Biafran war, in a refugee camp, buried in an unmarked grave, and one of the first things my father did after the war was to organize a belated funeral ceremony. And so I try to remind myself that my father would want things done as they are done. When my sisters Ijeoma and Uche were born while my father was at Berkeley in the 1960s, he and my mother decided to speak only Igbo to them. "We knew they would learn English, and we could not imagine having children who did not speak our language," he told me. My siblings and I were raised with a strong sense of who we were as Igbo, and if it was pride, then it was a pride so organic, so inevitable, that it felt no need to call itself pride. We just were. There is much I find beautiful in Igbo culture, and much I quarrel with, and it is not the celebratory nature of Igbo funerals that I dislike, but how soon they have to be. I need time. For now, I want soberness. A friend sends me a line from my novel: "Grief was the celebration of love, those who could feel real grief were lucky to have loved." How odd to find it so exquisitely painful to read my own words.

22

On the Zoom calls, we are flailing, unprepared, uninformed on practical things. It is also an emotional floundering. We have been so fortunate, to be happy, to be enclosed in a safe, intact family unit, and so we do not know what to do with this rupture. Until now, grief belonged to other people. Does love bring, even if unconsciously, the delusional arrogance of expecting never to be touched by grief? We stumble; we veer from an extreme forced cheer to passive aggressiveness, to arguing about where guests are to be served. Happiness becomes a weakness because it leaves you defenseless in the face of grief. It is a testament to my parents that each of the six of us feels individually, intimately, known and loved. And so we mourn differently. Yet "people mourn differently" is easy for the intellect to absorb, but for the heart it is much harder. I come to dread the Zoom calls, shrouded in shadow. The family shape is changed forever, and nothing makes it more poignant than to slide on my phone screen and no longer see the square with the word "Dad."

My mother says that some widows have come to tell her what the custom is. First, the widow will be shaved bald—and before she can continue, my brothers promptly say that this is ridiculous and not going to happen. I say that nobody ever shaves men bald when their wives die; nobody ever makes men eat plain food for days; nobody expects the bodies of men to wear the imprint of their loss. But my mother says she wants to do it all: "I'll do everything that is done. I'll do it for Daddy."

23

Imagine dreading a burial and yet longing for it to pass. We have settled on a date, 4 September, and the bishop has kindly agreed to say Mass. It will be a Covid-compliant ceremony: face masks will be required and guests will be served in the homes of various neighbors, to follow social-distancing rules. I am to draft the invitation. Writing "funeral" is impossible for me. My friend Uju types it because, at first, I cannot. But a day before we print, there are rumors that the Nigerian airports will no longer open in August. The news is haphazard—even basic information is uncoordinated—and it is all the more confounding because in neighboring countries the airports are open. Nigeria, as usual, making everything more difficult than it should be. The incompetence is iridescent, splaying, touching, tainting with its many-pronged evil shine. Disillusionment with the land of my birth has been my life's constant, but an animosity this astringent is new. I felt something like it only once before, when my father was kidnapped, in 2015, by a group of men in collusion with his driver, who told him to ask his famous daughter to pay the ransom. Of the men who threw him into the boot of a car and left him for three days in a forest, only his driver has been caught. I have never been as grateful for my father's dual Nigerian-American citizenship—thanks to my older sisters, who were born in America—as I then was. The Nigerian government was spiritless, while the American ambassador checked in and called and sent a counselor and a kind investigator, who coached my mother on how to talk to the kidnappers. And after Okey dropped off a bag full of cash under a tree in a remote area, my father was released, rattled but calm—that capacious thing in him again.

"They didn't pronounce your name properly, so I told them the correct pronunciation," he told me. He seemed visibly upset only when telling us how the kidnappers had said, "Your children don't love you," and how he had responded, "Don't say that, that is incorrect, don't say that about my children." After the kidnapping, my father said he could no longer live in Nsukka; he wanted to move to "the village," our ancestral hometown Abba.

"I don't ever want to be on that road again," he said of the pothole-riven way where the kidnappers had cut him off, and where his driver, pretending to be shocked, had stopped the car. The kidnapping brought out a new vulnerability in him, a vulnerability that was willingly laid bare, a softening of his carapace. With his vulnerability also came an old-man stubbornness, the occasional cantankerousness, which sometimes annoyed but mostly amused us.

And so 4 September is impossible. The Nigerian government announces that the airports will open in late August, and my mother returns to the church to get a new date. It is now 9 October. The next day a Nigerian newspaper reports that the government has said that the airport opening is tentative—maybe, maybe not. My mother is desperate for a firm date. "After the burial we can begin to heal," she says. I am heartsick to see her look so brave and so drained.

24

The waiting, the not knowing. All over southeastern Nigeria, mortuaries are full because the coronavirus has delayed funerals. It doesn't matter that this mortuary is supposed to be the best in Anambra State. You still have to visit often and tip the morticians; there are horror stories of loved ones being brought out of mortuaries looking unrecognizable. Every week, Okey goes to check on things and emerges wounded. It is as if every week he witnesses again this so fiercely unwanted transubstantiation. I have to brace myself to hear. Or I don't want to hear. "Maybe stop going?" I suggest to him. "Let's get somebody not close to us to go." And Okey says, "I'll go every week until we are able to lay him to rest. Daddy would do the same for any of us."

25

One night, in a vivid dream, my father comes back. He is sitting on his usual sofa in the living room in Abba, and then at some point it becomes the living room in Nsukka. The hospital made a mistake. What about my brother Okey's visits to the mortuary? Also a case of mistaken identity. I am ecstatic, but worried it might be a dream, and so, in the dream, I slap my arm to make sure it is not a dream, and still my father is sitting there talking quietly. I wake up with a pain so confounding that it fills up my lungs. How can your unconscious turn on you with such cruelty?

26

My mother tells a story of my father, in our university house in Nsukka in the 1980s, jumping out of the bath and dashing, still wet, to his study because he had finally figured out a problem. He loved academia but not its politics. "When I was made deputy vice chancellor," he told me, "I couldn't wait to leave all the squabbling and get back to teaching." He studied mathematics at Ibadan, Nigeria's premier university college, then affiliated with the University of London, and when he went to Berkeley, to do a PhD in statistics, on a USAID scholarship, he felt his British training was at odds with the American way. He faltered. He decided he would leave the program and return to Nigeria, but his adviser, Eric Lehmann, encouraged him, telling him that he, too, had come to the U.S. with British training. "He was a very kind man," my father said often, one kind person admiring another. He and my mother were once asked to dinner at Lehmann's home, and they dressed up in Nigerian *abada*, and on the way a little boy pointed at my father and said, "He's wearing funny clothes"— a story that still amused my father decades later.

He returned to Nigeria with my mother and my sisters shortly before the Biafran war started. In that war, all his books were burnt by Nigerian soldiers. Mounds of charred pages in a pile in my parents' front yard, where they once grew roses. His colleagues in America sent him books to replace those that were lost; they even sent him bookshelves. I remember my father telling me how much he admired the great African-American mathematician David Blackwell, and in my novel *Half of a Yellow Sun*, a character whose books have been lost in the Biafran war is sent books from America, with a note that reads, "For a war-robbed colleague, from fellow admirers of David Blackwell in the brotherhood of mathematicians." I now do not remember whether I made up that line or whether my father got a similar note. Perhaps I made it up, moved by the image of all those academics in America coming together to support my father, a colleague robbed by war.

In 1984, my father taught for a year at San Diego State University, and he spoke fondly of his friend Chuck Bell, an African-American academic who helped him get settled. One day, he recounted, Chuck Bell opens the fridge in my father's apartment to get something to drink, sees a crate of eggs and shouts, "Jim!" My father, alarmed, asks what is wrong, and Chuck Bell says, "You can't eat eggs. They'll kill you—too much cholesterol. You must throw them away now."

My father told this story wryly, as if to say, "Of all the things to tell me not to eat!" and "Who knows what Americans will come up with next!"

"You can't eat eggs!" I'd say to my father at breakfast as he peeled a boiled egg or spooned egg sauce onto a slice of yam.

27

⟋

I last saw my father in person on 5 March, just before the coronavirus changed the world. Okey and I went from Lagos to Abba. "Don't tell anyone I'm coming," I told my parents, to ward off visitors. "I just want a long weekend of bonding with you two."

The photos from that visit make me weep. In the selfies we took just before Okey and I left, my father is smiling, and then laughing, because Okey and I are being goofy. I had no idea. I planned to be back in May for a longer visit, so that we could finally record some of the stories he had told me over the years about his grandmother, his father, his childhood. He was going to show me where his grandmother's sacred tree had stood. I had not known this part of Igbo cosmology: that some people believed that a special tree, called an *ogbu chi*, was the repository of their *chi*, their personal spirit. My father's father was kidnapped in his youth by relatives and taken to be sold to Aro slave traders, but they rejected him because of a large sore on his leg (he walked, my father said, with a slight limp), and when he returned home, his mother looked and saw that it was him and, crying and screaming, ran to her tree to touch it, to thank her *chi* for saving her son.

My father's past is familiar to me because of stories told and retold, and yet I always intended to document them better, to record him speaking. I kept planning to, thinking we had time. "We will do it next time, Daddy," and he would say, "Okay. Next time." There is a sensation that is frightening, of a receding, of an ancestry slipping away, but at least I am left with enough for myth, if not memory.

28

On 28 March, my favorite aunt, my mother's younger sister Caroline, died suddenly of a brain aneurysm, in a British hospital that was already locked down because of the coronavirus. A joyous woman. We were stunned by sadness. The virus brought close the possibility of dying, the commonness of dying, but there was still a semblance of control, if you stayed home, if you washed your hands. With her death, the idea of control was gone. Death could just come hurtling at you on any day and at any time, as it had with her. She was perfectly fine one moment, the next she had a very bad headache and the next she was gone. A dark time inexorably darkened. She had lived with my parents for many years before I was born, and, to my sisters, she was more a big sister than an aunt. I look back now at my father saying her death was "shocking," in a voice strained by that shock, and I imagine the universe further plotting sinisterly. In June, he would go, and a month later, on 11 July, his only sister, my Aunt Rebecca, heartbroken about the brother she had spoken to every day, would go too, in the same hospital as my father. An erosion, a vile rushing of floods, leaving our family forever misshapen. The layers of loss make life feel papery thin.

29

Why does the image of two red butterflies on a T-shirt make me cry? We don't know how we will grieve until we grieve. I don't particularly like T-shirts, but I spend hours on a customization website, designing T-shirts to memorialize my father, trying out fonts and colors and images. On some, I put his initials, "JNA," and, on others, the Igbo words "*omekannia*" and "*oyilinnia*"— which are similar in meaning, both a version of "her father's daughter," but more exultant, more pride-struck.

Have T-shirts ever brought such escape? Often, I pause to cry. Often, I think about what he would think of them. He viewed my interest in fashion, especially my less conventional choices, with an accepting amusement. He once said, of a pair of wide balloon-cut trousers I wore to an event, "*Nke dika mmuo.*" This one looks like a masquerade. "Masquerade" is perhaps not the word I might have chosen, but I did see his point. He would approve of some of these T-shirts, I think. It is design as therapy, filling the silences I choose, because I must spare my loved ones my endless roiling thoughts. I must conceal just how hard grief's iron clamp is. I finally understand why people get tattoos of those they have lost. The need to proclaim not merely the loss but the love, the continuity. *I am my father's daughter.* It is an act of resistance and refusal: grief telling you it is over and your heart saying it is not; grief trying to shrink your love to the past and your heart saying it is present.

It does not matter whether I want to be changed, because I am changed. A new voice is pushing itself out of my writing, full of the closeness I feel to death, the awareness of my own mortality, so finely threaded, so acute. A new urgency. An impermanence in the air. I must write everything now, because who knows how long I have? One day, Okey sends a text that reads, "I miss his dry humor and how he would do a funny little dance when he was happy and how he would pat your cheek and say 'never mind.'" It makes my heart leap. Of course I remember how my father always said "never mind" to make us feel better about something, but that Okey has remembered it too makes it feel newly true. Grief has, as one of its many egregious components, the onset of doubt. No, I am not imagining it. Yes, my father truly was lovely.

30

I am writing about my father in the past tense, and I cannot believe I am writing about my father in the past tense.

Chimamanda Ngozi Adichie is the best-selling author of the award-winning novels *Americanah, Half of a Yellow Sun,* and *Purple Hibiscus;* the story collection *The Thing Around Your Neck;* and the nonfiction *We Should All Be Feminists* and *Dear Ijeawele, or A Feminist Manifesto in Fifteen Suggestions.* A recipient of a MacArthur Fellowship, she divides her time between the United States and Nigeria.

A NOTE ON THE TYPE

This book was set in a version of the well-known Mono-
type face Bembo. This letter was cut for the celebrated
Venetian printer Aldus Manutius by Francesco Griffo, and
first used in Pietro Cardinal Bembo's *De Aetna* of 1495.

The companion italic is an adaptation of the chan-
cery script type designed by the calligrapher and printer
Lodovico degli Arrighi.

Composed by North Market Street Graphics
Lancaster, Pennsylvania

Printed and bound by LSC Communications
Crawfordsville, Indiana

Designed by Anna B. Knighton